Date: 5/1/17

J 796.323 ERV
Ervin, Phil,
Total basketball /

TOTAL
BASKETBALL

BY PHIL ERVIN

SportsZone

An Imprint of Abdo Publishing
www.abdopublishing.com

abdopublishing.com

Published by Abdo Publishing, a division of ABDO, PO Box 398166, Minneapolis, Minnesota 55439. Copyright © 2017 by Abdo Consulting Group, Inc. International copyrights reserved in all countries. No part of this book may be reproduced in any form without written permission from the publisher. SportsZone™ is a trademark and logo of Abdo Publishing.

Printed in the United States of America, North Mankato, Minnesota
102016
012017

THIS BOOK CONTAINS
RECYCLED MATERIALS

Cover Photos: Alonzo Adams/AP Images, foreground; Shutterstock Images, background
Interior Photos: Shutterstock Images, 1; Charles Krupa/AP Images, 4–5; Ed Wagner/ Chicago Tribune/MCT/Newscom, 6; Eric Risberg/AP Images, 9; AP Images, 10–11, 40–41, 54–55; MPPL EMPICS Sports Photo Agency/Press Association/AP Images, 13; Jeff Chiu/AP Images, 14–15; Rick Bowmer/AP Images, 16; Jessica Hill/AP Images, 18–19; Al Behrman/AP Images, 20; Ray Chavez/Bay Area News Group/TNS/Newscom, 23; Gene Herrick/AP Images, 24–25; David Zalubowski/AP Images, 26; Gerry Broome/AP Images, 28–29; Kevin Reece/Icon Sportswire/AP Images, 30; Charlie Neibergall/AP Images, 32– 33; Carol Francavilla/AP Images, 35; Ed Reinke/AP Images, 36–37; Matt York/AP Images, 39; Bob Child/AP Images, 43; Stacy Bengs/AP Images, 44; Mark J. Terrill/AP Images, 46–47, 56; Matt Sayles/AP Images, 48; John Swart/AP Images, 50–51; David Rae Morris/ Polaris/Newscom, 53; Bill Kostroun/AP Images, 58–59; Steve Dykes/AP Images, 61

Editor: Patrick Donnelly
Series Designer: Jake Nordby

Publisher's Cataloging-in-Publication Data

Names: Ervin, Phil, author.
Title: Total basketball / by Phil Ervin.
Description: Minneapolis, MN : Abdo Publishing, 2017. | Series: Total sports |
    Includes bibliographical references and index.
Identifiers: LCCN 2016945423 | ISBN 9781680785029 (lib. bdg.) | ISBN
    9781680798302 (ebook)
Subjects: LCSH: Basketball--Juvenile literature.
Classification: DDC 796.323--dc23
LC record available at http://lccn.loc.gov/2016945423

CONTENTS

1   ANYTHING IS POSSIBLE 4

2   BASKET BALL 10

3   THE GREATS 14

4   INNOVATIONS....................................... 18

5   DYNASTIES 24

6   RIVALRIES 28

7   MARCH MADNESS 32

8   FOR LOVE OF COUNTRY............................ 36

9   WOMEN IN BASKETBALL 40

10   AROUND THE WORLD................................ 46

11   COACHING LEGENDS 50

12   PUTTING ON A SHOW 54

13   A BRIGHT FUTURE 58

GLOSSARY.. 62

FOR MORE INFORMATION 63

INDEX.. 64

ABOUT THE AUTHOR.............................. 64

ANYTHING IS POSSIBLE

Kevin Garnett paused to think about what the moment meant.

The superstar forward had spent 12 seasons with the Minnesota Timberwolves. He failed to win a National Basketball Association (NBA) championship there. Garnett finally won a title after he was traded to the Boston Celtics. They beat the Los Angeles Lakers in the 2008 NBA Finals. Garnett was asked for his thoughts afterward.

"Anything is possible," an emotional Garnett said. "Anything is possible!"

Kevin Garnett, *center*, can barely contain his joy after winning the NBA title with the Boston Celtics in 2008.

4

Michael Jordan celebrates after hitting the game-winning shot to clinch a playoff series against the Cleveland Cavaliers in 1989.

Basketball has been around 125 years. And it's true: practically anything is possible in the game.

The sport has seen many iconic moments. Players such as Michael Jordan have provided them. The former Chicago Bulls guard is one of the best players ever. He made a game-winning shot in the national championship game as a freshman in college at North Carolina. He did the same thing

16 years later in the 1998 NBA Finals. As a pro, Jordan scored 32,292 points. He also earned six NBA titles and five Most Valuable Player (MVP) honors. And he played in 14 NBA All-Star Games.

The National Collegiate Athletic Association (NCAA) has had its share of impossible moments, too. In 2006 tiny George Mason University made it to the Final Four. Along the way, the Patriots beat Connecticut and North Carolina, two of the top three teams in the nation.

Hall of Famer Wilt Chamberlain once scored 100 points in an NBA game. On March 2, 1962, the Philadelphia Warriors center made 36 of 63

LAKER LEGEND

Earvin Johnson earned his nickname "Magic." He did amazing things on the court. Johnson played 13 seasons with the Los Angeles Lakers. The point guard won five championships and three NBA MVP Awards. But his most impressive feat might have come at the end of his rookie year. Johnson started a game at center because Kareem Abdul-Jabbar was injured. But it wasn't just any game. It was Game 6 of the NBA Finals. Johnson scored 42 points as the Lakers beat the Philadelphia 76ers to clinch the title.

field-goal attempts. He also made 28 of 32 free-throw attempts in a 169–147 victory over the New York Knicks.

Today LeBron James is one of the NBA's greatest players. He's won the NBA MVP Award four times. He also won two championships with the Miami Heat. Then in 2016 he won a title with his hometown Cleveland Cavaliers.

The University of Connecticut women's basketball team won 11 NCAA titles between 1995 and 2016.

Golden State Warriors guard Stephen Curry has become a star, too. Curry's dad, Dell, played in the NBA. Stephen was considered too small to become an elite player. But he turned himself into a two-time NBA MVP and won the league title in 2016.

Basketball is one of the most popular sports in the world. As Garnett said, in this game anything is possible.

Superstar LeBron James, *right*, won the NBA championship with the Cleveland Cavaliers in 2016.

2 BASKET BALL

Dr. James Naismith invented basketball in Springfield, Massachusetts, in 1891. He wanted to create a game his students could play indoors during the cold New England winters. Peach baskets were hung at each end of the school's gymnasium. Naismith had students throw soccer balls into them. A man on a ladder retrieved the ball after a basket was made. Naismith wrote 13 rules for this new game. He called it "Basket Ball."

The first game was played in 1892. It featured nine players on each team. Today the game is played with five players per side. In 1894 Naismith

Dr. James Naismith, *center*, instructs members of the University of Kansas fencing club in 1930, almost 40 years after he invented basketball.

had a new ball to replace the soccer ball. Eventually the peach baskets were replaced with nets.

It didn't take long for the game's popularity to spread. Soon, American colleges began playing it. The Minnesota School of Agriculture and Hamline University squared off in St. Paul, Minnesota, in 1895. This is recognized as the first college game. A year later, Stanford beat the University of California-Berkeley in the first women's contest.

Professional basketball came along in the early 1900s. In 1949 the Basketball Association of America merged with the National Basketball League to form the NBA. The American Basketball Association (ABA) was a rival

FOUNDING FATHER

Dr. James Naismith was born in Canada. After inventing basketball, Naismith became the first head coach at the University of Kansas. He also was a minister and medical doctor. The Naismith Memorial Basketball Hall of Fame in Massachusetts is named after him. So are the Naismith Awards. They go to the top college player and coach for both men and women each year.

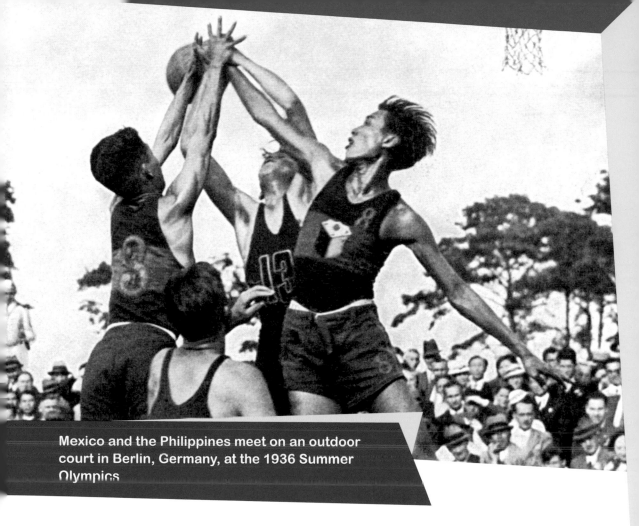

Mexico and the Philippines meet on an outdoor court in Berlin, Germany, at the 1936 Summer Olympics

league that began in 1967. When it folded in 1976, the NBA added four of its teams.

Today the NBA has 30 teams. Approximately 350 schools play at the Division I level of the National Collegiate Athletic Association (NCAA). And there are thousands of smaller college, high school, and youth squads. Basketball is played in gyms, on driveways, and in parks all over the world.

3

THE GREATS

The NBA has seen many superstar players. But few stand out like Michael Jordan. Jordan broke a slew of NBA records. His statistics are among the best ever. But his ability to perform in important games truly sets him apart.

That's what the best players do. Cavaliers forward LeBron James also has the rare ability to take over games. He scores, rebounds, and defends so well the other team has a hard time recovering. Through his first 13 NBA seasons, James averaged 27.2 points, 7.2 rebounds, 6.9 assists, and 1.7 steals per game. He's been

Stephen Curry broke the NBA record for three-pointers in a season two years in a row.

Hakeem Olajuwon, *left*, battles with Patrick Ewing in the 1994 NBA Finals.

even better in the playoffs. James led his teams to six straight NBA Finals from 2011 to 2016, winning three of them.

Stephen Curry changes quarters, games, and playoff series, too. The Warriors guard is an outstanding shooter, ball-handler, and passer. He often defends the opposition's top point guard. In 2015–16 Curry broke his own NBA record for three-pointers made in a season.

Many greats of the past influenced the way the game is played today. Kareem Abdul-Jabbar was a star in the 1970s and 80s. He remains the league's all-time leading scorer. Other big men changed the way basketball is played with their size and athleticism. Wilt Chamberlain, Bill Russell, Patrick Ewing, and Hakeem Olajuwon were some of the best centers ever. Kobe Bryant is one of the top crunch-time players ever to step on a basketball court.

KING JAMES

LeBron James went straight from high school to the NBA. The Cavaliers made him the first pick in the 2003 draft. James left for Miami in 2010. He led the Heat to a pair of NBA titles. Then he returned to his home state and the Cavaliers in 2014. Two years later he led the Cavs to their first NBA championship.

But none of them did it alone. Jordan had star teammates in Scottie Pippen and Dennis Rodman. James has Kyrie Irving and Kevin Love. Curry works well with Klay Thompson and Draymond Green. Bryant played with supersized big man Shaquille O'Neal. As great as each of those players is, basketball remains a team game.

4

INNOVATIONS

New rules, shifting strategies, and advancements in technology have helped change basketball over the years. The innovations began with cutting the bottom out of the peach basket. But they certainly didn't end there.

The NBA had a problem in the 1950s. This might sound strange, considering how fast-paced NBA games are today. But back then, basketball could be pretty boring. Teams often would stop trying to score if they had a lead. They just passed the ball around the perimeter to run out the clock.

The NBA's shot clock was so popular that it was adopted by many other levels as well.

88:28

28

1:23

24

UCONN
13

UCONN
3

VANGUARD

VANGUARD

In the 1953–54 season, NBA teams averaged fewer than 80 points per game. Today, scores are often in the hundreds. What happened? In 1954 the NBA adopted a 24-second shot clock. Teams had to shoot within 24 seconds of getting the ball. Otherwise, the other team got the ball back. The shot clock sped up the pace of the game. More shots meant more scoring. And teams hustled the ball down the court rather than walking it up slowly to kill time. The game became much more entertaining.

On November 22, 1950, the Fort Wayne Pistons beat the Minneapolis Lakers 19–18.

The three-point line was another big change. The ABA was the first league to make this rule popular. The NBA didn't adopt the three-point line until 1979. College and high school leagues soon followed.

The three-point line is closer to the basket in some levels of the game.

The three-point line wasn't the only big change resulting from the NBA-ABA merger. Many ABA teams employed more creative offensive strategies. The league had a culture that made entertaining fans a priority. The NBA eventually took a similar approach. That helped form it into the league it is today.

LONG SHOTS

Today's best teams tend to shoot a lot of three-pointers. The Golden State Warriors and Cleveland Cavaliers are two such teams. They ranked in the top four of three-pointers taken and made in 2014–15 and 2015–16. Those two teams met in the NBA Finals both seasons.

Professional and college basketball games are less physical than they used to be. Rules are tighter. Referees are quicker to call fouls. Defenders have to be more careful.

New types of training and technology have made the game more advanced, too. New training programs have made players faster and stronger. The NBA Development League was founded in 2001. This league lets professional players get better before making the jump to NBA competition.

NBA officials are calling games more closely, despite the protests of players and coaches.

Teams also rely on technology to evaluate their players' performance. Tiny sensors can track players' movements during games. These provide a wealth of information. Teams can see how far players have run during a game. Statisticians also keep track of what kinds of shots players make or miss most often.

5

DYNASTIES

In ancient times, a dynasty was a series of rulers from the same family or group. In the sports world, a dynasty is a run of multiple championships by the same team.

Basketball has seen many dynasties. One of its most famous began shortly after the NBA's creation. Starting in the 1958–59 season, the Boston Celtics won eight championships in a row. No other major professional sports team has won that many consecutive titles. The streak was part of a remarkable 11 titles in 13 seasons. Hall of Fame point guard Bob Cousy, center Bill Russell, and

The Boston Celtics celebrate the first of their eight consecutive NBA championships in 1959.

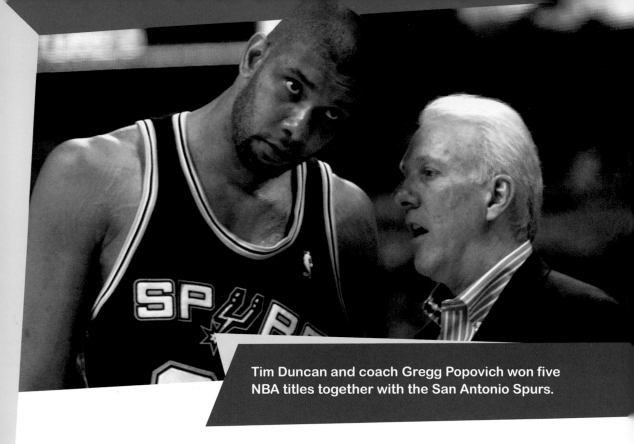

Tim Duncan and coach Gregg Popovich won five NBA titles together with the San Antonio Spurs.

coach Red Auerbach led Boston during that era. The Celtics led the NBA with 17 championships through 2016.

Connecticut coach Geno Auriemma has built a dynasty in women's college basketball. UConn won 10 championships from 2000–16. This includes four straight starting in 2013.

Legendary college coach John Wooden had a historic run at the University of California, Los Angeles (UCLA). His Bruins won 10 NCAA championships between 1964 and 1975. Four of those teams went undefeated.

UCLA wasn't the only dynasty in Los Angeles. The Lakers have had three separate dynasties. The Minneapolis Lakers won five league crowns from 1949 to 1954. Center George Mikan was the star of those teams. The Lakers moved to California in 1960. Kareem Abdul-Jabbar and Magic Johnson carried Los Angeles to five championships in seven NBA Finals appearances during the 1980s. In the early 2000s Kobe Bryant's Lakers won five championships.

But perhaps the most notable run aside from Boston came from Michael Jordan's Chicago Bulls. They won six NBA championships from 1991 to 1998.

SUPER SPURS

Some may not consider the San Antonio Spurs of the 2000s a dynasty. They are in the conversation of best NBA teams, though. In 1999 and 2003, coach Gregg Popovich, center David Robinson, and power forward Tim Duncan teamed up for a pair of championships. Popovich and Duncan went on to win three more, including the 2014 crown.

6

RIVALRIES

The University of North Carolina (UNC) and Duke University are eight miles apart. They play in the same conference. But they don't have much else in common. UNC is a public school. Duke is private. The Tar Heels have powder blue uniforms. Duke's Blue Devils wear a darker shade of blue. But the two teams love beating each other.

North Carolina-Duke is one of many great rivalries. The schools have combined for 35 Final Four appearances. Each had won five NCAA titles through 2016. The matchup features legendary coaches. They include Dean Smith and

The UNC-Duke rivalry is one of the fiercest in college basketball.

Magic Johnson, *left*, and Larry Bird were the faces of the Lakers-Celtics rivalry of the 1980s.

Roy Williams at UNC and Mike Krzyzewski at Duke. Star players Michael Jordan, Vince Carter, Grant Hill, Christian Laettner, and many others have been part of the rivalry.

Kentucky-Louisville is another exciting college rivalry. So are Purdue-Indiana and UCLA-Arizona. Students and fans highlight those games when the schedules are released.

Rivalries are a big part of the NBA, too. None is more prominent than the Los Angeles Lakers against the Boston Celtics. The NBA's two most storied clubs have met in the finals a record 12 times. Hall of Famers Larry Bird and Magic Johnson faced off in their prime. Their own individual rivalry helped the NBA become more popular in the 1980s.

Jordan and Detroit Pistons guard Isiah Thomas were individual rivals. They had many memorable head-to-head duels. So did centers Wilt Chamberlain and Bill Russell.

HOOSIER HYSTERIA

Indiana University and Purdue University are natural rivals. Both schools are in Indiana. Basketball is huge there. The state high school basketball tournament is an annual classic. The state's best players often go on to play at either Indiana or Purdue. Eight other Division I basketball programs provide plenty of opportunities in that basketball-crazy state.

7

MARCH MADNESS

The NCAA men's basketball tournament is also known as "March Madness." The final moments of the 2016 tournament showed why.

North Carolina guard Marcus Paige made an off-balance, double-clutch three-pointer. His improbable shot tied the championship game with only 4.7 seconds left. The Tar Heels needed one defensive stop to go to overtime.

But Villanova forward Kris Jenkins had other ideas. He made a long three-pointer as time expired. The Wildcats were national champs.

Kris Jenkins is nearly swallowed by the crowd after hitting a three-pointer to win the 2016 NCAA title for Villanova.

Earlier in that tournament, Texas A&M trailed Northern Iowa by 12 points with 44 seconds left. But the Aggies pulled off an amazing comeback to tie the game. Then they won it in overtime.

Every March, 68 Division I college basketball teams play for a national title. Every March, the unexpected happens. George Mason University's 2006 Final Four run is one example. In 2011 Virginia Commonwealth made the Final Four. Butler, a small Indiana school, made it all the way to the national championship game in 2010 and 2011.

Jenkins's buzzer-beater was just one of many famous shots in March Madness history. Valparaiso guard Bryce Drew

TRAILBLAZERS

One memorable NCAA tournament performance was also part of American history. The 1966 Texas Western team featured an all-black starting lineup. Kentucky was its opponent. The Wildcats didn't have any black players on their roster. Texas Western won 72–65. It was the first time a team with five black starters won a title. The Miners also were the only team other than UCLA to win the NCAA championship between 1964 and 1973.

Duke's Christian Laettner, *left,* takes his famous turnaround jumper that beat Kentucky in overtime in the 1992 NCAA East Regional Final.

made a similar three-pointer in the 1998 first round to beat Mississippi. Duke forward Christian Laettner's last-second, turnaround jumper beat Kentucky in 1992, putting the Blue Devils in the Final Four. North Carolina State forward Lorenzo Charles's memorable buzzer-beater was a dunk. He put in a teammate's missed shot as time ran out in the 1983 national championship game.

8

FOR LOVE OF COUNTRY

Basketball was introduced to the Olympics in 1936. Women's basketball was added as an event in 1976. The US men's team has won 14 gold medals. The US women's team has won gold in all but three Olympics.

Until 1992 only amateurs were allowed to compete in Olympic basketball. That meant the US roster was always composed of college players. NBA stars had to stay home. That rule changed for the 1992 Summer Games in Barcelona, Spain. NBA legends known as the "Dream Team" represented the United States that year.

US coach Chuck Daly, *center*, talks strategy with members of the Dream Team at the 1992 Summer Olympics.

Michael Jordan, Larry Bird, Magic Johnson, and other superstars easily won the gold medal in Barcelona. That team is considered the best collection of talent ever assembled on one roster.

The United States has typically dominated at the Olympics. There have been upsets, though. In 1972 the Soviet Union beat Team USA in a controversial finish at the gold-medal game. And Argentina upset the United States in 2004.

In 2016 Team USA continued its usual dominance in both Olympic basketball tournaments in Rio de Janeiro, Brazil. The US men's team won its sixth gold medal in the previous seven Olympics. The US women's team won for the eighth time in nine Olympics at the Rio Games.

Carmelo Anthony throws down a dunk at the 2016 Olympic Games.

9
WOMEN IN BASKETBALL

Women have played basketball almost as long as men have. It just took longer for them to gain a foothold in the world of athletics.

Physical education teacher Senda Berenson introduced the game at Smith College in Massachusetts in 1892. She had read about the game recently invented by Dr. James Naismith. She taught it to her students. Its popularity spread throughout the country. Women's teams were as common as men's teams at American colleges and universities. But society soon frowned on women competing in athletics. Teams were disbanded.

Members of the Smith College women's basketball team scrimmage in 1904.

Most of the country forgot about women's basketball for decades.

Widespread interest in the game began to pick up again in the early 1970s. A new law called Title IX took effect. It required universities to offer the same athletic opportunities to women as they do to men. Soon women's basketball was back on college campuses. In 1982 the NCAA began sponsoring women's basketball.

The University of Connecticut has dominated the women's college hoops scene. Legends such as Maya Moore, Diana Taurasi, Sue Bird, and Rebecca Lobo played there. But UConn isn't the only powerful college program. Baylor, Notre Dame, Texas A&M, and Tennessee all

TENNESSEE TITAN

Connecticut Coach Geno Auriemma is considered by many to be the greatest women's college basketball coach ever. But former Tennessee coach Pat Summitt isn't far behind. Summitt coached the Lady Vols from 1974 to 2012. Her teams won eight national championships. When Summitt retired in 2012, she had 1,098 career victories. This was the most of any basketball coach ever.

Diana Taurasi is one of many UConn players who cut down nets after championship victories.

have had successful teams. Tennessee is the only team other than Connecticut to win three straight NCAA titles.

On the professional side, a few leagues had come and gone by the time the Women's National Basketball Association (WNBA) was formed in 1997. The Houston Comets were the WNBA's first dynasty. Guard Cynthia Cooper, guard/forward Sheryl Swoopes, and forward Tina Thompson formed the club's core. Houston won the first four WNBA championships. Thompson retired as the league's all-time leading scorer.

The most recent WNBA dynasty belongs to the Minnesota Lynx. Minnesota's trio of forward Moore, guard Seimone Augustus, and point guard Lindsay Whalen won championships in 2011, 2013, and 2015.

The circumference of a WNBA basketball is approximately 1 inch (2.5 cm) smaller than that of an NBA ball.

Cooper, Swoopes, and Thompson were among the league's early pioneers. So were Los Angeles Sparks center Lisa Leslie and New York Liberty center Lobo.

More recently, Bird teamed with Australian center Lauren Jackson to lead the Seattle Storm. The Phoenix Mercury featured Taurasi and center Brittney Griner. Chicago Sky forward Elena Delle Donne won the WNBA MVP Award in 2015. And Tamika Catchings starred for the Indiana Fever.

Maya Moore, *left*, and Seimone Augustus sparked the Minnesota Lynx to three WNBA titles in five years.

10

AROUND THE WORLD

Basketball's worldwide popularity has exploded since the 1990s. The NBA has millions of fans in Europe, China, India, and Africa. The league plays preseason games and some regular-season games in other countries. Games can be viewed in 215 countries and territories and are broadcast in 47 different languages.

The rise in popularity has led to an influx of international talent. In the 2015–16 season, 100 NBA players came from countries other than the United States.

Pau Gasol, *left*, and Dirk Nowitzki are two of the NBA's top European stars.

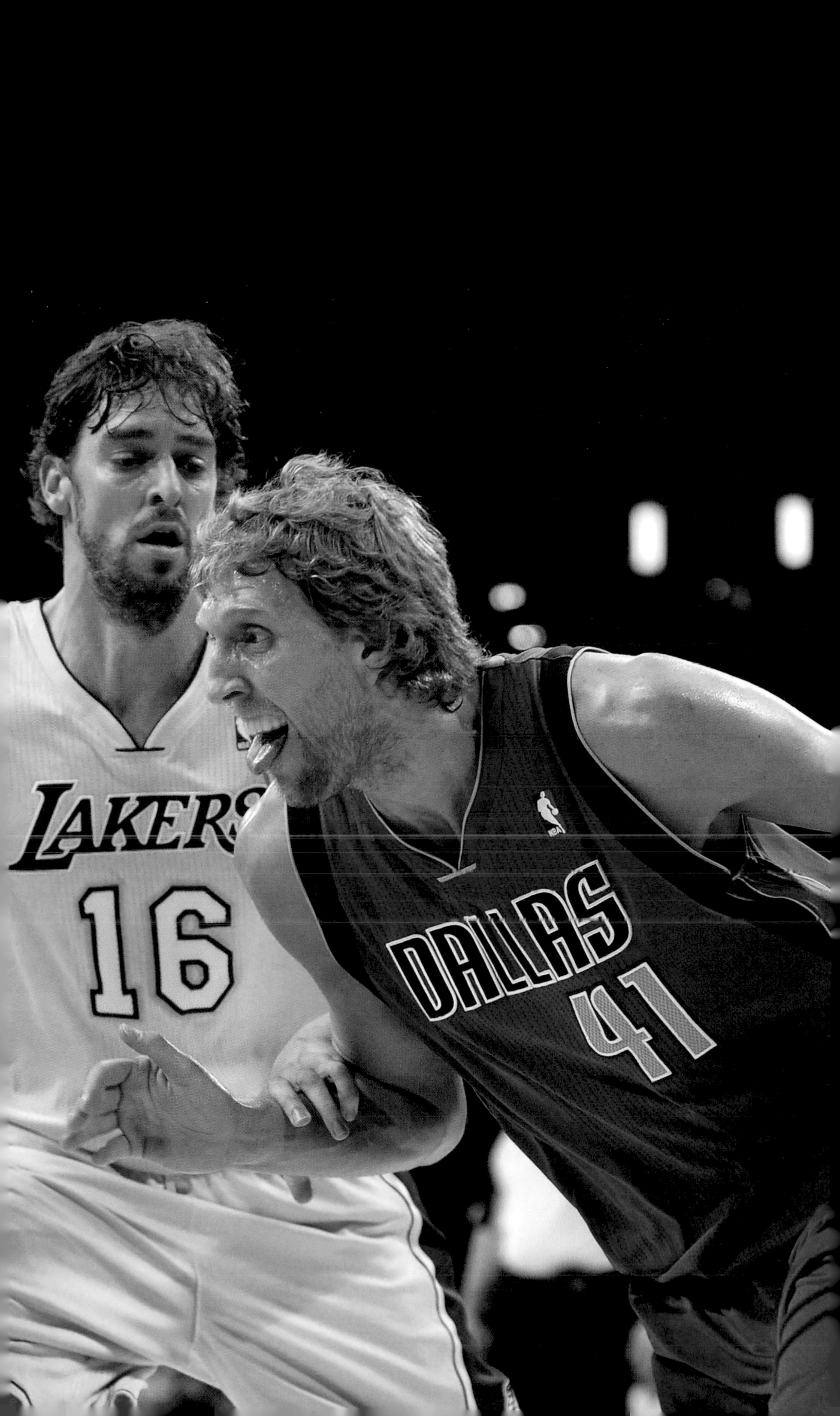
LAKERS
16
DALLAS
41

Yao Ming was an eight-time All-Star with the Houston Rockets.

Some of basketball's best players were born overseas. Hall of Fame center Hakeem Olajuwon came from Nigeria. He became the NBA's all-time leader in blocked shots. And he was just as good on offense. Olajuwon led the Houston Rockets to back-to-back championships in 1994 and 1995. San Antonio Spurs power forward Tim Duncan followed a similar path. The US Virgin Islands native was a five-time NBA champion. Dallas Mavericks power forward Dirk Nowitzki grew up in Germany. He led the Mavs to the NBA Finals in 2006.

The list of international stars is long. Former New York Knicks big man Patrick Ewing grew up in Jamaica. Atlanta Hawks small forward Dominique Wilkins and Spurs point guard Tony Parker were born in France. Phoenix Suns point guard Steve Nash is Canadian. All-Star center Pau Gasol is from Spain. Spurs shooting guard Manu Ginobili is from Argentina. Rockets center Yao Ming was the first Chinese star in the NBA. And legendary center Dikembe Mutombo came to the United States from the Democratic Republic of the Congo.

The International Basketball Federation (FIBA) was formed in 1932. It oversees international competitions including the Olympics. Russia, Spain, China, and many other countries have their own professional leagues as well.

NORTHERN EXPOSURE

The first NBA game was actually played in Canada. On November 1, 1946, the New York Knickerbockers beat the Toronto Huskies 68–66 in Toronto. The teams were part of the Basketball Association of America. The league later became the NBA.

COACHING LEGENDS

Phil Jackson knew a lot about basketball. He also knew how to motivate players. Jackson coached Michael Jordan and the Chicago Bulls to six NBA titles. Then he led Kobe Bryant and the Los Angeles Lakers to five more championships. No other coach has won 11 NBA titles.

Great coaches combine strategy with leadership. Red Auerbach mastered both as coach of the Boston Celtics. His teams won nine championships in 10 years. Later he stepped away from coaching to focus on being Boston's general manager. Auerbach won 938 games as a coach.

Phil Jackson twice led the Chicago Bulls to three straight NBA titles.

This marked a record at the time of his retirement. Fourteen of his players made it to the Hall of Fame. Thirty went on to become coaches.

Gregg Popovich began coaching the San Antonio Spurs in 1996. His teams won five championships through 2016. Popovich is a master at helping players get better. Many of them improved dramatically after joining the Spurs.

College basketball has seen legendary coaches, too. Former UCLA coach John Wooden is regarded as one of the best leaders in any sport. His philosophy on life, which he called his "Pyramid of Success," has been used by teams and businesses all over the world.

Duke coach Mike Krzyzewski has more victories than any other NCAA Division I men's coach.

COACHING STYLES

Some basketball coaches use distinct styles of play. Some prefer zone defense. Others prefer their players to run the floor and shoot quickly. Phil Jackson was famous for the triangle offense. In this offense, three players stand in a triangle on one side of the court. The other two work on the opposite side. The strategy is designed to give players open shots.

Pat Summitt was a legend on the sidelines for the Tennessee Lady Vols for nearly 40 years.

Syracuse's Jim Boeheim, longtime Indiana coach Bob Knight, and North Carolina's Dean Smith also rank high on that list.

Tennessee's Pat Summitt leads all women's coaches in victories with 1,098. A few veteran coaches are threats to pass Summitt before they retire. They include longtime Stanford coach Tara VanDerveer and North Carolina's Sylvia Hatchell. C. Vivian Stringer of Rutgers and UConn's Geno Auriemma are also contenders.

12

PUTTING ON A SHOW

Basketball is a competitive sport. It takes a lot of hard work and skill to succeed. But it's also a game. It's supposed to be fun.

That's why the NBA has events such as its annual All-Star Game. It features the best players in the league each season. Former Lakers great Kareem Abdul-Jabbar made the All-Star team 19 times. Lakers guard Kobe Bryant was selected 18 times. High-flying forward Julius "Dr. J" Erving made 16 appearances.

Kareem Abdul-Jabbar, *left*, battles Julius Erving for a rebound in the 1977 NBA All-Star Game.

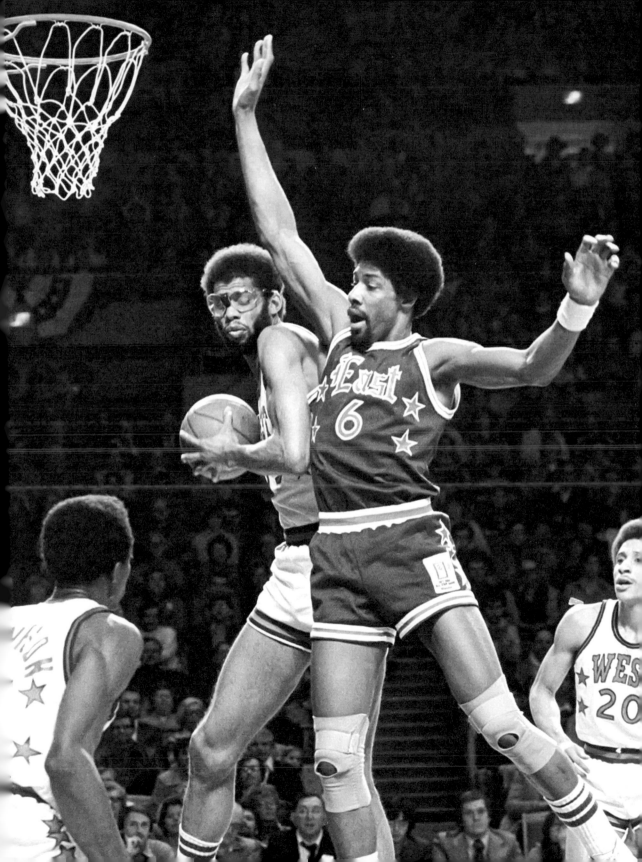

Nate Robinson shows his stuff at the 2007 NBA Slam Dunk Contest.

The same weekend, basketball's best dunkers show off in the NBA Slam Dunk Contest. New York Knicks guard Nate Robinson is the only three-time winner of the event. Also during All-Star Weekend, other skills competitions let players show off their shooting, dribbling, and passing abilities.

The NCAA, WNBA, and high school basketball all have their own All-Star Games and skills competitions. And the Harlem Globetrotters are basically a traveling All-Star show.

They play exhibition games and perform tricks on the court. The Globetrotters thrill fans around the world.

The Naismith Memorial Basketball Hall of Fame is a place where fans can learn about the game's past. The best players and coaches from men's and women's pro and college basketball are enshrined there. The Hall is located in Springfield, Massachusetts. That's where Dr. James Naismith invented the game.

The National Collegiate Basketball Hall of Fame is in Kansas City, Missouri. It focuses on men's college basketball. The women's game has its own Hall of Fame in Knoxville, Tennessee. International basketball stars are honored at the FIBA Hall of Fame in Madrid, Spain.

HOLLYWOOD HEROES

Basketball's entertainment value goes beyond the court. The sport is the topic of many movies. Some even feature NBA players. Basketball films include *Space Jam*, *Blue Chips*, *Like Mike*, *Hoosiers*, and *Glory Road*. Basketball players also appear frequently in commercials. They endorse different products, including basketball shoes and equipment.

13

A BRIGHT FUTURE

Many young basketball players dream of hearing their name called during the NBA Draft. But only a few get to experience it. Most players enter the league through the draft. They get there by doing well in high school and college. Scouts watch them during this time. If a player is good enough, teams will try to select him in the draft.

Minnesota Timberwolves teammates Karl-Anthony Towns and Andrew Wiggins know what it feels like to be drafted high. They were the first overall picks in 2014 and 2015, respectively. Each won the NBA Rookie of the Year Award.

Former NBA commissioner David Stern congratulates Anthony Davis after the Hornets chose Davis with the first pick of the 2012 draft.

Today's NBA features many exciting players. Golden State Warriors forward Kevin Durant looks to be on his way to a Hall of Fame career. Rockets shooting guard James Harden is one of the league's most dynamic players. Point guard Chris Paul and forward Blake Griffin lead a strong Los Angeles Clippers team. And back-to-back NBA Finals matchups featuring LeBron James against Stephen Curry in 2015 and 2016 were wildly entertaining. James's Cleveland Cavaliers and Curry's Golden State Warriors each won an NBA title in that stretch.

Players today are bigger, faster, and stronger than those of the past. But the basics of the game remain unchanged. Teams with good defenses win. And no

ONE AND DONE

Some star players came straight out of high school into the NBA. Timberwolves power forward Kevin Garnett was one of the first to do so. Kobe Bryant and LeBron James did, too.

Today players must wait at least one year after their high school graduation to turn pro. The best NBA prospects play a year of college basketball. Then they enter the draft. They are part of the so-called "one and done" movement. Towns and Wiggins are examples.

Minnesota forward Karl-Anthony Towns is one of the NBA's many exciting young players.

matter how good an individual player is, basketball remains a team game.

The sport's worldwide popularity is likely to keep growing. The Internet and social media allow fans to pay closer attention to their favorite teams and players than ever. Millions watch college and pro games on television. And millions more play the game, whether they're just having fun or competing for championships.

The game of basketball has a colorful, exciting past. And its future looks even brighter.

GLOSSARY

amateurs
People who are not paid to perform an activity.

crunch time
The final moments of a game in which the score is close.

Division I
The highest level of collegiate athletics.

double-clutch
A move in which a player changes the position of the ball in midair while shooting.

draft
A system that allows teams to acquire new players coming into a league.

exhibition
A game that doesn't count in the standings.

general manager
A team employee responsible for negotiating contracts with that team's players.

innovation
Something new or different.

perimeter
In basketball, the area near the three-point line.

professional
A person who gets paid to perform an activity.

roster
A list of players who make up a team.

FOR MORE INFORMATION

Books

Frisch, Nate. *The Story of the Golden State Warriors.* Mankato, MN: Creative Education, 2015.

Norwich, Grace. *I Am LeBron James.* New York: Scholastic Paperbacks, 2014.

Williams, Doug. *Great Moments in Olympic Basketball.* Minneapolis, MN: Abdo Publishing, 2015.

Websites

To learn more about basketball, visit **booklinks.abdopublishing.com**. These links are routinely monitored and updated to provide the most current information available.

INDEX

Auriemma, Geno, 26, 42, 53

Berenson, Senda, 40
Bird, Larry, 31, 36
Bird, Sue, 42, 45
Bryant, Kobe, 17, 27, 50, 54, 60

Chamberlain, Wilt, 7, 17, 31
Curry, Stephen, 8, 16–17, 60

Duncan, Tim, 27, 48

Garnett, Kevin, 4, 8, 60
Ginobili, Manu, 49
Griner, Brittney, 45

Irving, Kyrie, 17

Jackson, Phil, 50, 52
James, LeBron, 8, 14, 16–17, 60
Jenkins, Kris, 32, 34
Johnson, Magic, 7, 27, 31, 36
Jordan, Michael, 6–7, 14, 17, 27, 30–31, 36, 50

Krzyzewski, Mike, 30, 52

Mikan, George, 27
Moore, Maya, 42, 45

Naismith, James, 10, 12, 40, 57

Olajuwon, Hakeem, 17, 48

Popovich, Gregg, 27, 52

Russell, Bill, 17, 24, 31

Smith, Dean, 28, 53
Summitt, Pat, 42, 53
Swoopes, Sheryl, 43, 45

Taurasi, Diana, 42, 45

Whalen, Lindsay, 45
Wooden, John, 26, 52

ABOUT THE AUTHOR

Phil Ervin was born and raised in Omaha, Nebraska. In addition to writing sports books, he has covered sports for FOX Sports, the *St. Joseph* (Missouri) *News-Press*, and *Forsyth County News* in Cumming, Georgia. Phil attended Benedictine College in Atchison, Kansas.